50 BIGGEST MISTAKES
I SEE INFORMATION
MARKETERS MAKE

BRET RIDGWAY

NEW YORK

50 BIGGEST MISTAKES
I SEE INFORMATION MARKETERS MAKE

by **BRET RIDGWAY**
© 2011 Bret Ridgway. All rights reserved.

ISBN 978-1-60037-867-6 (paperback)

Library of Congress Control Number: 2010937586

Published by:

MORGAN JAMES PUBLISHING
The Entrepreneurial Publisher
5 Penn Plaza, 23rd Floor
New York City, New York 10001
(212) 655-5470 Office
(516) 908-4496 Fax
www.MorganJamesPublishing.com

Cover Design by:
Heather Kirk
Heather@BrandedForSuccess.com

Interior Design by:
Bonnie Bushman
bbushman@bresnan.net

In an effort to support local communities, raise awareness and funds, Morgan James Publishing donates one percent of all book sales for the life of each book to Habitat for Humanity.
Get involved today, visit
www.HelpHabitatForHumanity.org.

ACKNOWLEDGMENTS

This book would not have been possible were it not for the support of many people. As you create your information products it's important to remember that you will not do it alone. One player does not make a winning team.

First, to my business partner and the co-founder of Speaker Fulfillment Services, Bryan Hane, thank you. Your focus on the operations and management side of the business allows me to do the creative marketing and product development that are more fun for me.

To my original mentor and an entrepreneur to his very core, Craig Hane, another heartfelt thanks. Your faith and trust in me has seemingly never wavered over the years even when there were times I really doubted myself.

To all the members of the AM2 Platinum family, thanks for your input into helping bring this course to fruition. While I stress that an information product doesn't have to be perfect, it does have to be good. And your contribution definitely made the *50 Biggest Mistakes* better then it would have been.

And, finally, to my family, you're at the base of it all. None of this would be possible without your ongoing support. To Karen—my wife of 23+ years and my children Christina, Jacob and Mitchell. I love you all more than words can say and am so proud of all of you for being the wonderful people that you are.

Bret Ridgway

WHAT INFORMATION MARKETERS ARE SAYING ABOUT

"THE 50 BIGGEST MISTAKES"

"Bret Ridgway's new book *The 50 Biggest Mistakes I See Information Marketers Make* is one of the most valuable resources on information marketing I've ever run across.

And it shouldn't be a surprise. After all, as co-founder of Speaker Fulfillment Services, the go-to place almost ALL top info marketers turn to for product fulfillment) Bret is in the unique position to witness firsthand exactly what works and what doesn't.

He can see, at a glance, on the shelves of his warehouse, who is selling and who is struggling. If you follow the advice Bret lays out in this book, and avoid making these 50 mistakes (actually 52 because he snuck a couple bonuses in there), the impact to your bottom line will be incredible.

Just after reading the first handful of 'mistakes' I've already made changes to an upcoming product launch I'm doing that should put an extra five figures into my pocket. (You need this book just so you can avoid mistakes #1 and #5 alone!) Bottom line ... I give this book my highest recommendation."

— **Eric Graham**
ConversionDoctor.com

"I must admit I was skeptical when I first heard about your *50 Biggest Mistakes* course. I've seen so many of these things about different topics and I thought it would be just like some of the others where they had very little content and it seemed like they were stretching just to hit a number like 50.

To my surprise it was jam packed with all sorts of things that could seriously sabotage a project. I was really impressed with your vast knowledge of the Information Product business. I can tell you know this industry inside and out. Your book really is sort of a survival guide.

I'm going back through many of my past projects and I'm following up with many of your suggestions. Oh by the way, thanks for throwing in those extra resources towards the end. Those are REALLY helpful."

— **Tracy Childers**
TracyChilders.com

"When it comes to the information marketing business, no one has seen more marketers, more products, and more seminars than Bret Ridgway. I mean, after all, he has a bird's eye view—whether running the sales table in the back of the room, chatting with his many contacts, or co-founding a very successful fulfillment company. When Bret speaks people stop, listen and take notes.

50 Biggest Mistakes is packed full of logical practical, and actionable advice, that anyone in the industry can take to the bank. The best way to fix a mistake is to avoid it in the first place. Bret's information will arm you with the knowledge you need to make that happen.

I highly recommend it and hope you'll pick up yours today."

— **DJ Dave Bernstein**
HiFiWebGuy.com

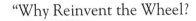

"Why Reinvent the Wheel?

Wouldn't you hate to put all that sweat and blood into an information product and have it fail miserably or at best never reach anywhere near its potential because you made a number of easily avoidable mistakes?

Wouldn't it be great to know the likely mistakes you were about to make and have a chance to correct them before they go out?

Now you can. You can now get a list of the biggest mistakes information marketers make. You can quickly scan the list, skip the parts you got right, and when you see a big mistake you were about to make, you could read the detailed discussion of how to fix it.

Bret Ridgway has created this course with extremely detailed advice of how to correct each of these common mistakes. Reviewing this list and resolving each potential mistake should be a routine step for all information marketers before they launch. It should also be used with existing campaigns.

Bret's broad and varied experience of seeing thousands of successful as well as failed information products gives him a rare insight that benefits his readers. Bret really cares and you can tell when you meet him as well as when you read his book.

Buying this book is a no-brainer for all information marketers. Luckily, Bret didn't take his own advice and made his #5 mistake. He did not charge anywhere near the value this product provides. Before he changes his mind, I would just buy it."

— **James Lange**
RothIRA-Advisor.com

"When Bret Talks, I Listen.

Bret has a unique 'behind the curtain' view of the top info marketing businesses ... including almost ALL of the top 'gurus'. Think about it.

Who else has access to this kind of information? Nobody but Bret. So, when he told me he was publishing the *50 Biggest Mistakes*, I knew it would be required reading. I was right.

So, just how valuable can one eBook be? Well, Bret's observations on Mistake #6 saved me three months on product development ... #13 made me over #300,000 ...

#16 will make a HUGE difference in sales for almost any product (or service) ... a recent New York Times Best Selling author used #24 to test the title of his book ... #38 is building my list for me like crazy, on autopilot ... are you getting the idea?

When Bret Ridgway talks about Information Marketing, I listen. You should, too!"

— **Ray Edwards**
RayEdwards.com

"As a true 'insider' in the information marketing industry, Bret provides tips and insights no one else can offer. He is truly uniquely qualified to write this book.

Just the product launch checklist is worth more than the price of the book! This is a MUST HAVE resource for everyone selling a CD, DVD, home study course or any other info product."

— **Jeanette S Cates, PhD**
TeleseminarBasics.com

TABLE OF CONTENTS

INTRODUCTION

Way back in 1992 I had the fortunate privilege of attending Gary Halbert's *"Hurricane Andrew Seminar"* in Key West, Florida. Little did I know at the time how that event would change my life and the interesting paths down which it would lead.

It's fascinating to me how someone can track a line back from a specific event to another event to another event and know exactly how they got to the point that they're at today.

This book is a direct result (or maybe I should say an indirect result) of that event that happened about 15 years ago. Of course, there were specific things that occurred, which even led me to being in Key West those few years ago, but for the purposes of this story that's where it all began.

Gary Halbert's seminar was my first exposure to the world of direct marketing outside of the world of telemarketing, which I had been involved with for about ten years. But over the course of those few days back in 1992 I had the wonderful opportunity to learn from masters like Gary Halbert, Ted Nicholas, Bill Myers, David Deutsch, Brad and Alan Antin and many others.

It's also where I had the opportunity to meet Carl Galletti for the first time. That chance meeting led to a joint venture with Carl two or three years later where I took over Carl's hard-to-find marketing books catalog. You can still find this catalog on-line today at MarketingClassics.com.

Fast forward to 1999. Carl decided to put on his first Internet Marketing Superconference in Las Vegas and asked me if I would come out and set up a marketing bookstore at his event and handle the back-of-the-room sales. I had only a vague idea of what that entailed but it sounded like a great opportunity to learn and meet some new folks so I agreed to come out and help Carl.

That one event evolved into the eventual formation of Speaker Fulfillment Services as we know it today. And it's still evolving. Some of the speakers at Carl's event, who were event promoters in their own right, saw what we were doing and asked us if we could help at their event.

As we were handling these events we got to know many of the speakers very well. They knew we were doing product fulfillment because we were selling information products ourselves in various markets. Finally, at one of Carl's conferences well-known Internet marketer Jim Edwards cornered me and asked me if we would take over some fulfillment for him as it was becoming too much of a hassle to handle himself.

We'd been pondering it for a while, because it was a natural outgrowth of the relationships that had been established in the Internet marketing and information marketing communities.

So, in the spring of 2003, Speaker Fulfillment Services was officially formed and we began to offer product duplication and fulfillment services to information marketers. Because of the solid relationships that already existed in this market, we were fortunate to be able to work early in our history with great marketers like:

- Alex Mandossian
- John Childers
- Armand Morin
- Fred Gleeck
- Jeff Mulligan
- Mike Filsaime
- Alexandria Brown
- And many others

Over the last few years we've had a great window to view what information marketers are doing well, and what they're not doing so well. We've seen some great new product launches and we've seen some great products shrivel up and die because mistakes were made that could have been avoided.

This book has been put together to help you avoid these mistakes and increase your chances of successfully building your own information marketing empire.

Bret Ridgway

FOREWORD

Warren Buffett is the world's greatest investor (and a multi-billionaire) for one reason: he avoids mistakes. As the story goes, Mr. Buffet took a $100 investment and turned it into one of the most successful multi-billion dollar companies in the world.

Yet, if you had been given 30 seconds to ask him how he rose to the pinnacle of his profession, his answer to you would probably be his two rules of investing:

"Rule No.1 is never lose money. Rule No.2 is never forget Rule No. 1!"

These two rules have also governed my business philosophy. By simply avoiding the most common information marketing mistakes I have been able to turn my annual income into a monthly income in less than three years.

The central principle I am really talking about here is "winning by not losing." When you avoid mistakes that you or others make in any industry, you will WIN by not losing your money, your time and the confidence you need to reach the pinnacle of your own Info Marketing niche.

That's why the book you're now holding in your hands is critically important to your success. All 50 Information Marketing mistakes Bret Ridgway reveals can be avoided. You can avoid them ... and so can your competitors.

Yet, all 50 mistakes are still being made by both new and even veteran Info Marketers every single day, all over the world. So if one of your Info Marketing goals is to crush your closest competitors, you can practically do it by default if you eliminate the mistakes from your marketing activities and communications!

Your passport to becoming a wildly successful Information Marketer boils down to doing the opposite of the 50 Mistakes you read about in this book. Period.

Whether it's Mistake #13 (Not attending live events to network) or Mistake #34 (Failure to apply any "stick" strategies) or Mistake #30 (Not accepting multiple payment methods), just do the opposite of each mistake, which Bret outlines in this book, and you WILL almost effortlessly become wildly successful ... overnight.

Look, if you find yourself working harder and harder and still not making the money or enjoying the time-freedom you feel you deserve, then chances are, you're making many of the 50 mistakes revealed in this wonderful book.

So study this book! Absorb its contents. Keep it close by during your business day because in less than a couple of hours, you will discover how to crack the code to making more profits faster, better and with less human effort!

The famous English writer of science fiction, H.G. Wells, once said: "Wise men learn by other men's mistakes, fools by their own." That's wisdom you can live by to accelerate the growth of your Information Marketing business.

And when it comes to the marketing wisdom of learning from others' mistakes, only Bret Ridgway has the credibility to write about it. That is because no one else has run so many product tables in the "back-of-the-room" at as many seminars and live workshops. No one else manages product fulfillment for so many successful Info Marketers.

You will even find a few surprises that Bret added as additional resources. For example, his Resource Rolodex (on the back few pages) is probably worth a hundred times the price you paid for this book!

My final words of encouragement are these: It is my hope that you're inspired, motivated and influenced to consume this book in "one sitting." It will take you less than a few hours out of your day, but what you learn will last you a lifetime of greater profits and more time-freedom with your business.

So go ahead ... flip through these pages. As you do, you will soon discover the *50 Biggest Mistakes* that Bret Ridgway has seen Information Marketers make so you too can start winning by not losing.

— **Alex Mandossian**, *CEO and Founder*
www.HeritageHousePublishing.com

MISTAKE #1

NO UPSELLS IN YOUR
ONLINE ORDERING SYSTEM

Millions of dollars are left on the table every year by information marketers who are not offering their customers one or more additional products during the online ordering process.

If you're not taking full advantage of this most opportune time to sell your customers more of what you have to offer, then you're a member of this club. This is NOT the club to which you want to belong.

If you only have a single product, then it makes it difficult to sell more of your own products or services to them. So find a complementary product or service that you can sell via an affiliate program. If you can't bundle it in on your own order page (maybe it's a digital product delivery direct from the author), then offer it on your online thank you page via an affiliate link.

Or, if your product is appropriate, offer an extended subscription at a reduced price or other quantity discounts to get more money from your customers now.

You can upsell (or cross sell) either more of your own product or someone else's product. I've seen upsell percentages as high as 90% on some products. That means 9 out of every 10 people who were offered the additional product took advantage of it. Obviously, that results in a very positive impact on your bottom line—at no additional sales costs.

I've also seen upsells work where the product being offered as the upsell was priced at 5x the price of the original product. Probably not the norm—but impressive nonetheless. Anything you're considering should be tested first to see what gets the best response, but what you can test is only limited by your own creativity.

Upsells are powerful. Use them.

MISTAKE #2

NO RIDE ALONG OFFERS WITH YOUR PHYSICAL PRODUCT SHIPMENTS

This may surprise you, but out of several hundred clients that we've worked with over the last several years a total of just two—that's right I said two—take advantage of their product shipments to include additional marketing literature to try and stimulate additional sales.

You're already paying the shipping costs to send out your information product. What is the additional cost to you to have some "ride along" literature? It's simply the cost of printing some paper.

Let's take a look at this. You've got an excited customer who has just received your product. Time and time again it's been shown that the person most likely to buy from you is someone who has purchased before. So why not provide them an additional opportunity to purchase more of your products and/or services at a prime buying time?

You could include any one or more of the following in your outgoing product shipments:

- Sales flyer
- Product catalog

- Sample of a subscription newsletter
- Price sheet
- Testimonials from clients about other products/services you offer

Just be sure your ordering process is thoroughly thought out. If you're driving them to a website to order, make sure everything is fully tested and functioning as it should. If you're using a toll-free order line, make sure your scripts are written and they're ready to take orders for you.

Ride along offers can be a powerful weapon in your information-marketing arsenal. Make sure you take advantage of it.

MISTAKE #3

TRYING TO DO YOUR OWN PRODUCT DUPLICATION AND FULFILLMENT

If you're an information marketer and your business is up and going at all, you can quickly find yourself wearing any or all of these hats:

- Marketer of Your Information Products
- Public Speaker
- Marketer of Your Speaking Services
- Information Product Developer
- Shipping Clerk
- CD/DVD Duplicator
- Binder Assembler
- Customer Service Manager
- Order Taker
- Travel Planner

So you've got to ask yourself which of these hats you should be wearing. Where should you be applying your time and efforts to maximize your information marketing business?

When you're starting out, you probably should do it all yourself. You need to have an understanding of what is involved in producing and delivering your products to your customers. But, if your business is growing, you'll quickly find out that too much of your time is being spent on the mundane tasks—copying binders (or running down to the local quick print shop), duplicating CDs and labeling them one at a time, packaging things together, putting things in boxes, running down to the post office or UPS, etc.

This means you're probably not spending your time where you get the biggest bang for your buck—marketing your products and services and creating additional products. When is the right time to outsource your duplication and fulfillment requirements?

Ultimately, you'll have to decide when that time is for yourself. But what do you value your time at? $100 per hour, $200 per hour, more? Then how long does it make sense for you to be spending your time doing $10 or $20 per hour tasks?

If you're spending an hour per day running products to the post office that's an hour you're not investing in your real bread and butter.

And what is your opportunity cost? The time you're spending on $10 an hour tasks is time that's lost forever.

When you're spending time working in your business rather than working on your business then opportunities will slip by without you even noticing them.

There is a time when outsourcing your duplication and fulfillment needs makes perfect sense—both from a time management and a financial standpoint.

When is that time right for you?

MISTAKE #4

NOT INVESTING SOME TIME EVERY DAY ON MARKETING

It's so easy each day to get bogged down in the little details of your information marketing business that you forget to invest any time in actually building your business.

Michael Gerber of "*The E Myth*" fame describes it as working in your business rather than on your business. The solution, according to Internet marketing legend Armand Morin, is what he calls "Five-Minute Marketing."

He makes sure he spends at least five minutes every day on some business-building marketing activity. Maybe it's an email promotion to his list. Or maybe it's a couple phone calls to potential joint venture partners to get a commitment to participate in an upcoming new product launch. Or maybe it's lining up an article writer to generate 50 new articles on information marketing.

It doesn't matter what it is as long as you're consistently applying some effort every day to activities that will help you to grow your business. If you have employees, then the development of processes and procedures will be critical to your long term success.

These are certainly business building activities. But these may or may not be marketing activities, so amongst the full complement of business building activities make sure you include something within the marketing realm. Your future success depends upon it.

Here's a quick list of marketing opportunities you might do:

- Post something to your blog
- Do an affiliate training call
- Send an email promotion to your list
- Write a new article and submit it to the article directories
- Call your top joint venture partners and get a commitment to help you promote an upcoming new product launch
- Send thank you cards to your biggest customers
- Be a guest speaker on a teleseminar or webinar
- Speak at a live event
- Submit a press release
- Schedule advertising in a suitable ezine
- Write a new sales brochure to include with all outgoing product fulfillments

This list is certainly not meant to be all-inclusive, just to stimulate your thinking. And "Five-Minute Marketing" doesn't mean you have to do it all yourself. If you're building a company, then have one of your team members handle the marketing responsibilities.

Just be sure someone in your organization is investing some time in marketing every day. Your long-term success depends on it.

MISTAKE #5

SELLING YOUR PRODUCT FOR TOO LITTLE

Most information marketers initially underestimate the value of their information. Even experienced marketers sometimes have this problem. They think, "Oh, they will never pay $297, or $497, or $1997 for my product."

People will pay gladly if you have information that they want. If you can help them solve some problem they have, they will happily fork over their money for a solution.

The people that make it in the information marketing business selling $19 eBooks are few and far between. Now I'm not saying there's anything wrong with a $19 eBook. It can be a great front-end product for higher-ticket items you sell.

But, if the $19 eBook is all you sell, then you have to move an awful lot of product to generate any serious revenue. It's a pretty tough row to hoe. You've got to have a back end product or products that people can purchase from you which brings in larger amounts of money, to be successful in this business.

The concept of the Lead Generation CD or DVD for $5.95 shipping and handling has become very popular. We're not talking about that. A lead-generation device where people are actually paying you something to get into your sales funnel is great. Upselling them via telemarketing into your higher end programs is a model that's proven to work, and if it fits into your business, I'd encourage you to do it.

The key though is that you have that higher ticket back-end product. You can actually make a small profit on each of the lead-generation discs, but that's probably not where your real profits lie.

Do NOT undervalue your information products. People will gladly pay for the specialized knowledge you can provide them.

MISTAKE #6

TRYING TO MAKE IT PERFECT

I don't know how many times I've seen it. Dozens? Hundreds? What is it? It is the repeated pushing back of a new product launch date because the developer feels the product isn't perfect.

Every "*t*" hasn't been crossed four times, every "*i*" dotted six times, and the 23rd edit isn't yet complete. It doesn't have to be perfect. It needs to be out in the marketplace generating sales and making you money.

Should it be professional? Sure. But you can always come out with a 2nd edition where corrections are made later on. Chances are it will never be perfect. Even though it's been read multiple times by you and others, some error will be missed.

You've got to overcome your perfectionism-induced procrastination and get your product out in the market. There's a lot of truth to the advantage of the first mover.

What happens if you sit on your product while you're trying to make it perfect and someone else comes out with a competitive product in the same niche?

Even if your product is superior, your competition has sucked up a lot of the cash that might have been yours by hitting the marketplace first. You should have moved more quickly.

Professional is required. Perfection is not.

MISTAKE #7

SELLING A PRODUCT THAT ISN'T YET FULLY DEVELOPED

This one tends to be a bigger problem for the platform speaker from what I've seen, than for anyone else. It can certainly be true of any information marketer, but here's what I've seen happen frequently from platform speakers.

They get the audience stirred up (in a good way), and folks are rushing to the sales table to order Speaker X's package. But the package includes some component(s) that aren't yet fully developed. According to the presentation, things will be ready to go within a couple weeks.

But, invariably, two weeks turns into a month. Then, a month turns into two months. You get the picture. Now people are getting antsy, and refund requests begin to pour in. It's not a pretty sight.

The solution —make sure you don't sell a product from the stage that isn't yet fully developed. If you absolutely must deliver a presentation where you're selling something that isn't completed, you had better at least make sure you have some component (either physical or digital) that can be delivered to the purchasers quickly to keep them happy until the remainder of the product is ready.

How does this apply to you if you're not a platform speaker? Pretty much the same way. If you're planning a specific launch date for your information product, work the dates backwards to determine when all the product development work needs to be completed.

If you think it's going to take a week to edit your audio or video, then you need to allot two to three weeks in your schedule. If you think it's going to take 10 days to finish up the writing of the manual, you had better plan on 20 or more.

We see it time and time again. Information marketers who don't plan properly who are scrambling at the last minute to get things to their fulfillment house to produce the product. This can mean delayed deliveries and rush charges for jobs, neither of which is desirable.

Whether you speak from the stage or not, be sure your product is ready to deliver when you're ready to sell it. Communication with your customers is critical. If you manage their expectations proactively, then you can minimize the potential harm from not having a product ready to go. But the keyword here is "proactively."

Better to just make sure it's done so you don't have to worry about it.

MISTAKE #8

NO "READ THIS FIRST" OR "GETTING STARTED" DOCUMENT TO GUIDE USERS

Picture this. You've created a fantastic new information product in your niche. You've invested hundreds of hours of sweat into developing your "big box" package that consists of 12 CDs, 5 DVDs, and a 400-page manual in a three-ring binder. You're very proud, and rightly so, of your product. It's one impressive course.

Now, picture this. Your course arrives at the door of your customer in a clean white 14" x 14" x 10" box. Your customer eagerly tears into the box and begins unpacking the massive manual and all the CDs and DVDs that make up the course. They're thinking, "Wow, this is great. But where do I begin."

There's so much great information in the product they simply don't know where to start. So they toss the items back in the box with the thought that they'll figure it out later when they have a few more minutes.

But those few minutes never seem to arrive. Then they realize that they're coming up on the 30-day refund window, so they haul the box down to the post office and ship it back for a refund. This is a scenario that is all too familiar to those who have been in the information marketing business for a while.

What can you do to help minimize the instances of this unpleasant scenario? The key is that you need to help your customers to consume your information. You need to tell them step by step how to go through your course in a logical manner to get the maximum value from it.

Don't leave it up to them to figure out.

You need to create some type of "Read This First" document or "Getting Started" guide that will quickly get them into your course to begin the "consumption" process.

I've seen this "Read This First" document done in both written format (a letter or booklet) or as a PDF file burned onto a disc. My recommendation is a printed document that will be the first thing they see when they open your box.

Let's face it; if you can't get people started on your course, then they can't finish it. This means the likelihood of them purchasing additional information products from you is significantly reduced. When you get them started quickly into your course, your refund rate will also be reduced.

This means more money stays in YOUR pocket.

A "Read This First" or "Getting Started" document is an important part of a successful course. Be sure to include one with your next information product.

MISTAKE #9

NOT TESTING YOUR ONLINE ORDERING SYSTEM PRIOR TO LAUNCH DATE

By and large, information marketers are notoriously bad planners. They have so many irons in the fire that they fail to think out all the steps ahead of time. Completing all these steps maximizes their chances for a successful new product launch.

One of the things you think would be obvious is to fully test your on-line ordering system, prior to launch date. Whether you're using 1ShoppingCart, our Red Oak Cart system, Infusionsoft, Full Partner, Google Checkout or any other system you've got to take the time to make sure your entire ordering process works exactly as you want it to.

Have you added the product(s) to your shopping cart system?

When they click on the order button does the proper order page come up with the appropriate upsell offers?

Does any order page audio play properly and is it the right audio message?

Does it take them to the proper thank you page?

If the product is digital, does your system generate the appropriate email notice on where to get their download?

You get the point. There are a lot of little things that can quickly screw up your customer's purchasing experience.

Make sure you invest the time up front to eliminate those potential problems. If you're supplementing on-line ordering with telephone orders, make sure whomever is handling the incoming calls has the proper scripts, answers the phone the way you want it answered, and has a foolproof method for transferring the order information to you or your fulfillment house.

The same holds true for any other methods you may use to accept orders. Make sure all your ordering processes work like a finely-tuned machine. The devil is definitely in the details.

Shopping Cart
Driving You Nuts?

MISTAKE #10

NO UNANNOUNCED BONUSES IN PACKAGE

Let's face it; almost everybody loves a pleasant surprise.

When your customer receives your package and opens it up, what better way to make them feel even happier about their purchase then by including some type of unannounced bonus in the package. It should be something of value that they weren't expecting.

Ideally, the bonus item will be complementary in some way to the product they purchased. For example, it doesn't make any sense to include a bonus book about Fly Fishing in a package with a Search Engine Optimization course. But a book about Pay Per Click Advertising might be an excellent fit.

The bonus item doesn't even actually have to be physical in nature. While an additional CD or DVD or a book might only cost you a couple dollars or so, there is a definite hard cost associated with that bonus item that your numbers might not support.

You could make the book an eBook or the audio or video downloadable and place nothing more than a sheet of paper in your box instructing them where to go online to get their free bonus eBook, audio, or video.

You could also gift them access to a membership site of yours for a limited period of time, say 60 days, at which time recurring billing would kick in if they didn't choose to cancel. Just be careful with this and make sure you're not in violation of any FTC rules.

Or, if you have an online catalog, a gift certificate towards their next purchase from your site. The bonus options are really only limited by your own creativity.

Free follow-up bonus teleseminars or webinars are becoming a popular bonus item for some information marketers. These types of bonuses can be scheduled to occur on a time-delayed basis after the original purchase date.

In fact, some clever marketers announce these bonuses soon after the initial purchase by the customer but schedule some of them to occur just after the end of the initial product guarantee timeframe.

Everyone I know loves an unannounced bonus, so come up with something to make your customers even happier.

MISTAKE #11

NO FOLLOW-UP AUTORESPONDER TO HELP PEOPLE CONSUME YOUR PRODUCT

Alex Mandossian is the first person I ever heard speak of the concept of "Product Consumption." And he's dead on target. If you can't get your customers to even consume your product, then your chance for refunds increase significantly, and the chance that that customer will buy more products from you decreases significantly.

Similar in concept to Mistake #8—No "Read This First" or "Getting Started" document—avoiding this mistake is essentially the application of online tools in the form of autoresponders to help your customers continue to move through your product in a positive manner.

Where the "Read This First" can help get them out of the gate, the autoresponder is your best ally to keep them moving forward after that first day. It's that friendly little nudge after they've received your product that will help the sale "stick" and is designed to provide that helpful reminder of how to best consume your course for maximum benefit.

It's important to get people started quickly and keep their momentum going. So it's fairly common to have daily autoresponder messages for the first week to ten days after the product purchase.

Product consumption is what it's all about. It's your job to provide your customers the utensils they need to help them to consume your information product.

MISTAKE #12

TRYING TO RELY ON THE SALE OF A SINGLE PRODUCT

If you've been involved in marketing for any length of time you've probably heard that the person most likely to buy from you is someone who has purchased before.

This is so true. But if you have only one product to sell a customer you've reached the end of that revenue stream quickly unless it's some type of recurring billing product.

I see a lot of information marketers who develop a single product for a market niche. Then they immediately go to another market niche and develop a product for that niche and so on and so forth. While I'm not against playing in multiple markets, I am against having only one product for each niche you're working in.

When you're always trying to get a new customer (since you have no repeat business), your cost of sale is higher. When you have a second and third and fourth product aimed at the same niche, your marketing costs for each additional product you're selling to that niche are effectively zero. It's simply a matter of emailing your customer list another offer they can take advantage of.

About a dozen years ago, I was involved in the development of a training CD for the plant engineering and maintenance market. The CD was on a highly technical topic. If memory serves me correctly, it was titled "*The Rolling Bearings Troubleshooter's Guide.*"

It was decided that the product would be marketed via the web. I knew that one product would not make a company. So I negotiated deals with several technical publishers and other training developers for related books and training CDs that would be of interest to the same folks who had purchased the Rolling Bearings CD. A website—www. MaintenanceResources.com—was created and several millions of dollars worth of products have been sold via that site over the last 15 years.

The additional products you have to offer a market don't even have to be your own product(s). You can offer related products from people that on the surface may appear to be competitors of yours. Find products on ClickBank that you can sell to your list.

People are thirsty for knowledge and many will purchase almost everything they find on a certain subject. If you have only one product to sell them you're leaving a lot of money on the table.

MISTAKE #13

NOT ATTENDING LIVE EVENTS TO NETWORK

Here's a list of well known information marketers—Alex Mandossian, Armand Morin, Jim Edwards, Carl Galletti, Mike Stewart, Perry Marshall, Fred Gleeck, Sean Roach, Michael Penland, Ryan Deiss, Christina Hills, Mike Filsaime, Stu McLaren, Brad Antin, Donna Fox, Paulie Sabol, Michel Fortin, Gary Ambrose, Keith Wellman, Jeanette Cates, Alexandria Brown, Brett McFall, Ted Ciuba, Tom Hua, Joe Polish and Ray Edwards.

Besides the fact that they're all Internet/information marketers and most are clients of Speaker Fulfillment Services, what do all these people have in common?

The entire list is of people that I first met at a conference or seminar— every last one of them. Yes, you can establish great relationships online.

But the people who you will become closest to and who will be most willing to help you build your information marketing business are those people who you've had a chance to meet face to face and establish a personal relationship with.

Your best joint venture partners, super affiliates, clients, etc. will come from the group of people who you've taken the time to get to know by being where they are. You can build an information marketing empire on your own. But it's a lot easier if you have relationships with the movers and shakers in the industry and the place you get to know these people are at live events.

If you're not attending two to three live events each year I believe you're truly stunting the growth of your information marketing business. Get to several events each year from promoters like Armand Morin, Mark Victor Hansen, Dan Kennedy and Bill Glazer, Michael Penland or any of the dozens of other marketing conferences that occur every year.

Now don't get carried away. There's a time for learning and networking and a time for doing. If you become a seminar junkie who never takes the time to apply anything you've learned, then all the relationships you've forged will be of no value.

MISTAKE #14

TRYING TO DO IT
ALL DIGITALLY

When the Internet caught on, information marketers began a mad rush to digitize all their products and eliminate their "big box" packages. Hooray! No shipping costs. No fulfillment to deal with. This is great.

One little problem, though. Sales numbers began to fall in some instances. People still wanted the physical product. They wanted something they could hold in their hands. They craved that feeling of the validation of their purchase by having something they could actually show their spouse or business partner.

It's kind of tough to show off a bunch of bits and bytes. So the pendulum is beginning to swing back in the other direction. Smart marketers are recognizing that they're leaving a lot of money on the table by not offering their customers physical versions of their products in addition to the digital versions.

This digital dilemma also applies to the marketing channels that top information marketers use. The superstars in the information marketing industry know that there's a whole world of offline people who are interested in their products. They understand that if they limit their marketing to emails and websites that great opportunities are being wasted.

Email is a great tool. But it shouldn't be the only tool in your arsenal. You need to figure out how to reach those people who would be interested in your products that aren't Internet savvy yet. Don't overlook offline tools like direct mail, postcards, trade journal advertising, etc. that can significantly contribute to your profitable bottom line.

MISTAKE #15

A LACK OF A CONSISTENT LOOK AND FEEL TO ALL YOUR PRODUCTS

Branding used to be the playfield of the big boys only—the Coca-Colas and the Budweisers of the world. Small marketers don't have the resources to spend money on building a brand.

The late, great Gary Halbert steadfastly said that every marketing piece you do needs to have a direct call to action—it needs to generate sales!

And he's right of course. But branding is much more than blowing big wads of cash on just throwing your name out in front of a bunch of people. In the information marketing world branding applies to your product packaging.

It applies to your email communications. It applies to your offline communications as well. People like to buy from people that they know and trust. People they're comfortable with.

If you're marketing information products and you change the look and feel of every product you come out with inside a specific niche, than you're continually creating an environment where your customers have to familiarize themselves with you again and again.

You want your customers to recognize something new you've come out with as yours just by the look and feel.

You want to have already crossed that first hurdle of building trust by having built a brand that people already recognize. Your product packaging should be consistent with the look of your website. It should be similar to the look of any previous products you've introduced to that niche previously.

Just remember that it's not all about product packaging. See Mistake #37 for a specific example of how messing with branding in an email communication impacted one marketer.

MISTAKE #16

NOT INVESTING A LITTLE UP FRONT TO HAVE SOME GRAPHICS CREATED TO GIVE YOU A MORE PROFESSIONAL LOOKING PACKAGE

Dan Kennedy and Bill Glazer are great marketers. In terms of the impact they have on the information marketing industry they are the standard by which all other information marketing gurus are judged. And rightfully so.

They also produce, in my opinion, some of the most "Plain Jane" looking materials that exist in the marketplace. It works for them because they're icons in the industry. They didn't invent information marketing, but it almost feels like they did.

So they can get away with the "Plain Jane" look. You, on the other hand, probably can't. We talked in the previous section about branding. You need to be thinking in the long term about building your information marketing business.

That means you need to create that look and feel that people will always associate with you. So you must invest some money up front to create a professional looking package that makes people want to take you seriously.

If their first impression of you is boy, this guy looks like an "amateur" then you've created a tremendous barrier to overcome. Your content might be great, but if people can't get past the unappealing packaging it doesn't matter how great your content is.

I experienced this several years ago first hand. I ordered an information product from a couple guys who I hadn't heard of before, but it sounded like their content could be of some value. What I received in the mail was a hodgepodge of poorly copied newsletters and other pages just thrown haphazardly into a mailing envelope.

The content may have been outstanding, but I couldn't get past my "Man, this looks like crap" initial reaction. To this day, it remains the only information product that I have ever returned for a refund.

Bottom line—you need to invest some money up front to create a professional appearance for your packaging if you want people to take you seriously.

MISTAKE #17

OVERPRODUCING ON AN INITIAL PRODUCT LAUNCH TO TRY AND SAVE A FEW CENTS ON THE PER UNIT PRODUCT COSTS

I've seen it time and time again, especially with new authors getting a book published for the first time. They become so consumed with getting the lowest possible unit cost on the printing of their new book they order 5000 copies right out of the gate.

So instead of paying $3.98 or $4.98 per book they get the unit price down to $2.98. Hooray, they saved a dollar or two per copy.

What happens next? 100 cases of books weighing 40 pounds or more each arrives at their home. They get stacked in the corner of the bedroom or in the garage, and there they sit, month after month after month. Sure, a few cases are opened and some books ship, but you're continually stepping around boxes and cursing yourself for ordering so many books.

You've tied up thousands of dollars in inventory that you hope you can sell. Hey, but you saved $1 or $2 per book.

If you're producing a "big box" package, you might also save some on the unit cost by producing more initially. But, unless you have a proven track record and can pretty accurately predict how many units you can sell, you're better off spending more per unit and having a lower quantity produced initially.

"Big box" packages can cost $30 to over $100 depending on what all is included in your package. So, you can conceivably tie up tens of thousands of dollars in production for units you hope you can sell—all because it saved you some money on the per-unit cost.

But what do you do if you sell more product than you expected? Have a plan in place to deal with your customers in case your product launch is more successful then you anticipated. If you ask your fulfillment house to produce 100 sets of a product for a launch and then you sell 300, you've created a potential problem you'll have to deal with to keep your customers happy.

Turnaround times for additional production can be several days or more. It is recommended you have some digital component to your package that people can begin to read or listen to right away while they are awaiting arrival of the physical package.

Or, if the package price justifies it, pull out a disc or small manual that can be shipped immediately to keep them happy until the "big box" arrives. Produce more of these up front than the full packages so you can immediately fulfill a portion of the package to all your customers.

It's primarily a matter of managing customer expectations.

If you keep your customers informed about the status of things proactively, you can significantly reduce any possible negatives that can result from having customers in a back order scenario.

MISTAKE #18

PACKAGING INCONSISTENT WITH THE PRICING OF YOUR PRODUCT

In the information-marketing world, you'll hear the phrase "perceived value" uttered frequently. Simply put, it means how much people think your product is worth. How you choose to package the information you're selling will have a tremendous impact on how your customers perceive its value.

Let's take a look at the relative perceived values of different products from lowest perceived value to highest perceived value. Keep in mind the content is identical regardless of the packaging.

Example 1: Single CD

LOW	→	MEDIUM	→	HIGH
Paper Sleeve		Jewel Case		DVD Style Case

If the CD is a free lead generation tool or a bonus item then a paper sleeve may be your best choice. The price that you're asking for the product will, to a large extent, determine what kind of packaging you want to utilize. If you're giving it away you may need to go bare bones on your packaging.

But, if the product is selling for $47, $97, or more than you need to dress up the package. It needs to be more impressive so a jewel case with full color inserts or a DVD style case with a full-color outsert will be called for. Remember, the content is identical. You are influencing perceived value of your content through different packaging.

Example 1: 100-page manual

LOW	→	MEDIUM	→	HIGH
Saddle Stitched		Perfect Bound		Three-ring Binder

Again, the content is identical in each of the formats. But the public has been conditioned to equate the value of a perfect-bound book with around a $19.95 price like you'd find in your traditional bookstore.

Put that same information into an 8½" x 11" spiral-bound document or a three-ring binder, then it appears to be more specialized knowledge. Therefore, people are willing to pay more for it.

If you're selling a multi-faceted product that consists of many CDs and/or DVDs and some printed materials, which will have a ticket price of $497 or higher, then you definitely want to stay toward the upper medium to high end of the perceived value scale.

How you choose to package the components of your information product is critical to how people will perceive its value. Be aware of the value scales above when you're deciding how you want your product to look.

If you want to charge a high price for your product, then be sure it's packaged professionally to increase the perceived value and substantiate the price you want to charge.

MISTAKE #19

NOT PROVIDING ADEQUATE SALES TOOLS FOR YOUR AFFILIATES

If you're going to be successful in the information marketing industry then a big key to your success will be lining up a strong group of affiliates to promote your products for you.

Every large new product launch within the last couple years that I'm aware of relied upon joint venture partners/super affiliates to drive traffic and generate sales.

But the regular ongoing sales of your products will also largely come from affiliates. In today's market affiliates literally have thousands of products from which they can choose to promote.

What most affiliates will do is promote those products that are easiest to promote. Of course, they want the large commissions. But, all other things being equal, they'll choose to promote the product for which the best affiliate tools are provided.

I'm certainly that way myself. Give me an email that all I need to do is tweak and I'll shoot an email out to my list. Ask me to write the email from scratch and it's just not going to happen.

So, what tools should you be providing? Here's a starter list (with kudos to my colleague and super marketer Alex Mandossian):

- Articles
- Banner Ads
- Text Links
- Affiliate Movie
- Email Teasers
- Ezine Ads
- Audio Billboards
- Testimonials
- Email Subject Lines
- Email First Sentences
- Training Calls

Any tool you provide should allow your affiliate to automatically generate what they need to use with their affiliate code already embedded inside.

Affiliates will be an important key to your information marketing success. Make sure you provide them with the best tools possible to give you a competitive advantage over others within your market niche.

A popular resource to create an affiliate toolbox:

affiliatetoolgenerator.com/affiliates/index.php?af=313136

MISTAKE #20

NO BUILT-IN NAME CAPTURE TOOLS INSIDE YOUR PRODUCT

When you develop any type of information product—a book, a CD, a comprehensive multi-media package, a home study course, or anything else—it's essential to build within your product, mechanisms to drive traffic back to your website to capture the name and email address of anyone that may see your product.

Products get passed around. So you don't know who all may be reading your information. If you've written a book that's being sold in a retail environment or via someone else's website then you probably have no way of knowing who has purchased your book. Barnes and Noble, Borders and Amazon certainly don't provide you this information.

So you've got to include something within that book that will cause the reader to come to your site and provide you with their name and email address. It can be a free bonus that can only be claimed online.

Or it can be a newsletter subscription they can only get online It doesn't really matter what it is—it just matters that you're capturing their information so you have the ability to market other products or services to them.

The same holds true for any other type of information product. If it's a CD put a sticker on the packaging to come and claim their free bonus at your site. If it's a home study course put the information on where to get that bonus within the content of your course. And do it several times within the product.

If it's an eBook you should have multiple links back to a specific website that will allow you to capture their information. Yes, even eBooks sometimes get passed around.

Your product should be a marketing tool. It's your job to make sure it is.

MISTAKE #21

NO RESEARCH TO CHECK THE VIABILITY OF YOUR DESIRED MARKET

Some people fall so in love with their idea for an information product they are totally oblivious as to whether a market even exists for that product.

Now, if you're truly passionate about a subject and you just want to write a book for your own self-satisfaction, that's fine. Go right ahead.

But if you're writing a book or developing a home study course, you'd better be sure that the market is even interested in your subject. So how do you determine the potential viability of a market?

The list below isn't all-inclusive, but it will give you some excellent starting points.

Examine the trade journals that serve your industry. Go to your local library and ask for their guide to periodicals. This will identify those magazines that serve your industry. Get a hold of some of their back issues by requesting their media kit. Look through the ads to see if similar products are being offered to your market. You can also pick up issues on the magazine rack at your local bookstore. You should subscribe to those publications that are in your niche.

Google your topic and research the Internet to see what competitive products already exist in the marketplace. Remember, competition is not a bad thing. If nobody is offering an information product on your subject you may have uncovered a hidden niche. But, more than likely, you've uncovered a niche that hasn't proven profitable so no one's playing in it.

Use online research tools like GoodKeywords.com or WordTracker. com to identify what keywords and keyword phrases people are searching for online. This will help you gauge the potential size of the market you're trying to reach. If very few people are looking for the subject you want to write about you've got a problem on your hands.

If you have an existing list, survey them using an online tool like ASKDatabase.com to see what level of interest they might have in your new subject. It's foolish to jump into a market blindly if you're entering that market with the thought of making money in it. Take the time to do your research in advance so you don't waste a bunch of your time and money chasing a market that doesn't exist.

MISTAKE #22

INSUFFICIENT INSTRUCTIONS ON HOW TO USE DISCS IF THEY AREN'T STRICTLY AUDIO

I just dealt with this specific issue recently for a client. I received a forwarded email from our client from a customer of his. "Hey, none of the discs play. They open up automatically to a main screen, and then nothing else happens."

So I pulled out the master discs and popped each of them into a computer to see what the issue was. It took me a few minutes to figure it out myself because there were no instructions in the product at all on how to play the discs.

In this particular case, they were videos on CD, and after the main screen came up you had to put your cursor over the subtitle on the screen and click it in order to launch the videos. Yet it didn't say that anywhere on the screen or in any support documentation.

Our client had to deal with a customer support issue that could have easily been avoided by including instructions on how to play those discs properly. Customer support is expensive.

Take a little time up front to develop the materials that will help people use your program most effectively. If they can't figure out how to play a video then you've got a problem on your hands.

Another component in this particular package was software discs with install links buried within a custom eBook program. The user needed to figure out on their own that the install links were accessible only by scrolling down within a certain section of the eBook. Again, a problem that could be avoided with better usage instructions.

You want people to "consume" your product. Give them the tools (instructions) they need to be able to do it.

MISTAKE #23

"WRONG" AUDIO FORMAT

We're an on the go society these days. It's important for you to know your market and understand fully how they want to consume your information.

If your client base includes a lot of people listening to your audio content during their commute time then make sure you provide them with your product in a format that is easiest for them to use.

We're frequently asked by clients if they should provide their audio in MP3 or WAV format for their users. I think the ideal answer is both, but that may not be practical from a cost or delivery standpoint.

If you are planning to deliver content on CDs to your customers then WAV format is still preferred. Why? Because most vehicle CD players are not yet MP3 compatible so MP3 formatted files will not be able to be listened to by your customers during their commute time.

This means they may be limited to listening to it on their computer. This is changing however, so within the next few years MP3 will become the standard for audio delivery.

As the popularity of iPods and other MP3 devices continues to escalate, both within vehicles and out, the need to deliver audio content in anything other than MP3 will all but disappear.

MP3 files are smaller than WAV files, so from a cost standpoint when going into a physical product you can deliver more content on less discs with MP3.

This may or not be good depending upon the perceived value you wish to create with your product. For now, your safest bet for delivery on CDs is a WAV file. For downloadable content then MP3 will definitely be your format of choice.

MISTAKE #24

NOT "BUYING" TRAFFIC TO TEST HEADLINES, OFFERS AND OTHER VARIABLES

In the old days, information marketers would draft their best headline, write what they felt was their best sales letter, and create their best offer. Then they'd mail their direct marketing piece and sit back and wait for the results to come in.

With the advent of the Internet, your ability as an information marketer to quickly test different headlines, copy, offers, and other variables has revolutionized the information marketing business.

Many software programs these days allow you to do split testing and multivariant testing to determine which combination will produce the best results for you. In addition, you can do this in minutes rather than the weeks it took in the old days to see what would work best.

It's important to do your testing quickly so you can optimize your overall results fast. The way you do this is by buying traffic to your website with Google AdWords.

You can have different versions of a site served up in rotation and monitor the results to see which is pulling best. You can't afford to assume you know what the winning headline will be. Or which offer will pull best.

There are literally hundreds of different variables you can test on your website. A couple of colleagues of mine—Michel Fortin and Eric Graham are experts on online testing and I'd encourage you to check out their knowledge of the subject. For more information on Michel and Eric, visit the Resources section of this book.

Also, your email software may also allow you to do split testing to determine what your "winners" are. For example, our own Red Oak Cart system allows users to segment their list and serve different versions of an email to each group to test which version draws the best response.

MISTAKE #25

TRYING TO DO IT ALL ONLINE— NOT TESTING OFFLINE MARKETING MECHANISMS

Many information marketers thrive in an online-only environment. If you're running a lifestyle business and it's just about generating enough revenue to let you play when you want to play, then that's fine. Online only may be perfect for you.

If it's about growing your information marketing business, then you've got to incorporate offline components in your marketing efforts, as well, to achieve the maximum desired results.

We talked in another section about how to research the viability of a potential market and how you can use trade journals in your research. You usually don't have to look hard at all in any industry publication to find lead generation ads for information products.

Several well-known information marketers have been offering "free" CDs or DVDs in offline publications to generate leads very effectively. When the Internet caught hold and email became so popular, the lure of "free" email drove most marketers to move their entire marketing effort online.

But there's so much money to be made by utilizing offline methods or a combination of offline and online—and smart information marketers understand they need to be playing in the offline world also.

Does it take a little bit more work? Sure it does, but if you want to build your information marketing empire, you need to be well versed in all aspects of direct mail and other offline methods. For resources in this area, please visit www.MarketingClassics.com.

MISTAKE #26

POOR PLANNING
FOR LAUNCH DATE

If you're planning a large product launch on a specific date, be sure to allow adequate time for everything involved in putting together a new product.

From graphics to overall packaging decisions to lining up affiliates to setting up your ordering mechanisms, there's a lot involved in successfully launching a new product.

I don't know how many times clients have come to our company, Speaker Fulfillment Services, just days prior to their intended launch date, and they're still editing audios or videos, don't have any graphics created yet, and any number of any other things that make it more difficult to meet a desired launch date successfully.

Here's a simple Product Launch Checklist that can help you plan better and increase your chances for a successful new product launch.

More than 2 Months Pre-Launch

- Create the content—record audio(s) and/or videos, write manual
- Determine what the product components will be—DVDs, Audio CDs, Data CDs, manuals, downloads, etc.

- If CDs or DVDs are included in the product, determine what packaging you want to use (individual DVD style cases, plastic sleeves in two or three-ring albums, paper sleeves, plastic sleeves included in print binder, jewel cases, other)
- If print components are to be included, decide on desired binding method (saddle stitched, three-ring binder(s) including size, spiral binding, comb binding, or perfect binding)
- Determine if tabs are to be included in printed component
- Determine if any components are to be shrink-wrapped
- Determine if printed components are to be printed single-sided or double-sided
- Determine if printed components are to be printed only in black or whether full color will be used.
- Determine if product will have any bonus items physical and/or download)
- Get pricing from your fulfillment company
- Begin lining up your affiliate and joint venture partners

Minimum of 8 Weeks Prior to Launch

- If transcripts are to be included, get audio transcribed
- Get artwork developed for all printed pieces (CD labels, CD/DVD packaging, binders, etc.)—if necessary, request specs from your fulfillment company
- Proof all artwork
- Determine desired audio format for final product (.wav or MP3 files)
- Inform your fulfillment house of launch date and the quantity to be produced
- Develop a product assembly document for your fulfillment company
- Provide your fulfillment company with a primary and back up contact to reach if there are any questions about the product
- Continue work on affiliate and joint venture partners

- Begin development of your affiliate tools including pre-written classified ads, articles, banners, etc.

Minimum of 6 Weeks Prior to Launch

- Format transcripts into final "print" version (PDF or Word document)
- Proofread your transcripts and other written documents
- Send transcripts and other written documents to your fulfillment company
- Quality check your audios and/or videos
- Write a thank-you letter to be included with the product
- Write a "Read this First" or "Getting Started" document to include with the product to help your customers consume your product
- Send all artwork to your fulfillment company via disc or downloadable links
- If appropriate, convert MP3 files to .wav format
- Break audio into tracks and add front/back music if desired
- Send your fulfillment company your physical address where a sample product can be shipped
- Write the sales copy for your website
- Develop your website
- Send physical masters of CDs and/or DVDs to your fulfillment house

Minimum of 4 Weeks Prior to Launch

- Determine preferred shipping method and notify your fulfillment company
- Proof a product mockup
- Notify your fulfillment company if the mockup is approved or if changes need to be made
- Add the product to your online shopping cart

- Inform your fulfillment company of any product name(s) the product may be sold under and accompanying SKU numbers
- If required, pay deposit on job to your fulfillment company
- Continue work on affiliate and joint venture partners

Minimum of 2 Weeks Prior to Launch

- Setup and test your order notice delivery mechanism with your fulfillment company

Launch Date

- Make website live

Post Launch

- If your launch exceeds expectations notify your fulfillment company of additional production requirements

MISTAKE #27

WORKING ON MULTIPLE PRODUCTS SIMULTANEOUSLY— DELAYING REVENUE GENERATION FROM ANY OF THEM

As an information marketer, you'll have no shortage of great ideas. Oh, if I only had as many minutes in a day as I have great ideas.

Here's what typically happens to many information marketers when they're first starting out. They do some research and determine they have viable products they can develop in multiple markets. So they begin writing an eBook or developing a course on chinchilla farming, raising cacti, earthworms, and who knows what else all at the same time.

Their thought process is like this. "I'll just work a little each day on each of my eight projects, and before long, I'll have a great big library of information products that I'll be making money on."

So they work a little while each day on their chinchilla-farming book. Then they switch over to their book on raising cacti. After a while, they tire of that, so they begin some work on their great new eBook on earthworms. And so on and so on.

By utilizing this approach, you delay the completion of any individual project for some period of time. So nothing's making you any money because everything is always in a constant state of development.

If each project takes a man month to complete, you're effectively delaying any possible revenue inflow until at least four months down the road if you're working on four projects simultaneously.

And, invariably, something that you think will take a week ends up taking two or more. So maybe those four months becomes six or seven or eight. You're hemorrhaging cash, and nothing is coming in.

What's a better plan? Focus on one and get it done. Get it out in the market to begin generating you revenue. Then move on to the second project and repeat the process. That way you have one project generating revenue after month one, another generating revenue after month two, another generating revenue after month three, etc. …

No waiting until month four to get anything coming in at all. That's if you're doing all the work yourself.

Experienced information marketers know they don't have to do all the product creation themselves. They use ghostwriters and other resources to help them generate more products more quickly.

This is where you want to get to. Just be sure when you're starting out you don't get sucked into the multiple project trap.

MISTAKE #28

FAILURE TO REPURPOSE CONTENT

A hot phrase these days in the information marketing industry is "repurposing content." In their course *"Repurposing Secrets"* Jeff Wark and Lori Steffen offer 216 different ways they say you can reuse and repurpose your information to drive traffic, add subscribers, increase sales, have more time and more money.

Alex Mandossian points out that one of the best examples of repurposing content is the hard cover book *"The Greatest Direct Mail Sales Letters of All Time"* by Richard Hodgson. Richard took all the sales letters he accumulated from friends and colleagues during the middle of the 20th century and compiled them into a book that sells for $129 on the www.MarektingClassics.com website.

Even though it's a hot topic right now, repurposing of content has been around forever. It's just that today there are newer technologies and additional media formats that your content can be put into.

Repurposing content allows you leverage your time more effectively by getting multiple uses out of something you do once. It allows you to reach a larger audience with your message. You can take the same core material and tweak it to make it applicable to different niches.

Here are just a handful of different formats and uses for repurposing of your content:

- Articles
- Audios
- Blogs
- Books
- eBooks
- eCourses
- Home Study Courses
- Membership Sites
- Podcasts
- Press Releases
- Special Reports
- Teleseminars
- Tips Booklets
- Transcripts
- Videos

Here's 7 additional repurposing secrets graciously contributed by the incredible Dynamic Duo of Content—Jeff Wark and Lori Steffen.

Offer a sample of your teleseminar product. This is a very effective technique for repurposing teleseminars that is definitely underutilized. For example, if you are selling a single teleseminar or a series of teleseminars, provide on the opt-in page or sales page a sample.

Offer it in streaming format so people can listen right there and then. You develop trust because you are willing to show people exactly what the product is like. It helps to build the relationship with them because they are receiving a free sample and if you are in the sample audio, they have the opportunity to hear your voice and connect with you.

Create an audio version of your eBook. Seven out of ten books purchased never get read. Many people are interested in the topic but too busy to ever sit down and read the book. Creating an audio version is easy and inexpensive; all the effort of the content for the book is already done and all you do is repurpose it into audio.

Related to number one is offering samples of your free teleseminars. You can post a sample of your teleseminar on your opt-in page and offer the complete teleseminar recording in exchange for their opt-in. If you regularly do free teleseminars, let them know that if they opt-in they will also be notified of future free teleseminars.

Combine posts from your blog to repurpose your blog posts into article content. If you want to create a 750 word article, put together three blog posts of 200 words each. Two hundred words are not that many—tips one through three above total over 200 words. Copy and paste the blog posts into a text editor, add an introduction and close, tweak the content a bit and you have an article ready for submission. You've accomplished two distinct tasks, blogging and article writing, with one effort by repurposing the blog into articles.

Here's another way to repurpose your teleseminar. Post either a sample of the entire teleseminar on your blog. Your blog is probably getting visitors that your other site or sites are not. Give those visitors the same opportunity to hear what you have to offer.

Make additional use of your articles by repurposing them as content for your autoresponder.

To emphasize why teleseminars are so valuable, this last tip will be one more way to repurpose your teleseminars. When you are going to a seminar or other networking opportunity, have some physical CD's of your teleseminar to hand out. It will get much more notice then just handing out a business card. When people see you handing out CD's they will often come to you to find out what you are giving away. Decide based on the size of the event and your budget how many you want to hand out.

Then have post cards or business cards to hand out when you run out and on it include the URL where they can get a downloadable copy for themselves or a free copy of a physical CD if they pay for the shipping and handling.

Everybody is working with limited time. If you have to write everything you generate from scratch, you're placing a tremendous burden on yourself.

Repurpose your content to optimize your time usage.

MISTAKE #29

TRYING TO DO TOO MUCH ON A SINGLE WEBSITE

Speaking legend John Childers often says, "A confused mind never buys." During his popular speaker training workshops he counsels speakers to make only one offer from the stage. Otherwise, you'll create confusion in your audience and they'll end up choosing nothing rather than selecting between two or more options.

The same framework should be applied to your website. As a general rule you should have only one product offered on an individual website. If you offer ten different products each should have a site of its own so the only choice the visitor has on that page is buy-no buy and not what to buy.

A confused mind doesn't buy. Now, we're not saying you can't have a catalog or corporate type of site in addition to each of the individual product sites. Many information marketers use their personal blog as their corporate site with links to each of their individual products. But this is in addition to an individual site for each product that sells that product and that product alone in the sales copy.

We're also not saying that you don't offer an upsell opportunity to a buyer once they've reached the ordering phase of your sales process.

But you're inserting this opportunity to purchase more into the process only after they've made the decision to buy and are in the checkout phase of the process.

Every website you have should have a clearly thought out objective. What do you want them to do when they come to that site? If that objective is to have them purchase some product of yours then don't incorporate other elements into the sales page that can distract them from your primary objective.

For example, a lot of links to external resources they may find interesting. If they click away from your site, there's a great chance that they're not coming back. Don't even provide that outlet for them. If you must have a link to another site, be sure it opens in a new window and leaves your primary information on their screen in a separate window. If you follow the "One Website—One Product" mantra, then you'll improve your online results significantly.

Pick up your copy of Bret Ridgway and
Frank Deardurff's new book
"The 50 Biggest Website Mistakes" at:
50BiggestWebsiteMistakes.com

MISTAKE #30

NOT ACCEPTING MULTIPLE PAYMENT METHODS

Here's the general rule—the more payment options you offer your prospect, the more sales you'll make. But many new information marketers fall into the trap of doing what's easiest for them and not making it as easy as possible for their customers.

It's been shown time and time again that if you offer credit card payment options, you will have more sales. Visa and MasterCard sales account for 85 to 90% off all credit card transactions, so that's where you'd want to start.

But there are purchasers who use only Amex or Discover cards. So you'll want to get them set up at some point in time. The temptation of some information marketers to slap up a PayPal-only option for payment is sometimes tough for them to resist. And, if your business is primarily a coaching practice or you're selling only a small number of high priced products then only offering PayPal may be a viable option.

You should definitely offer PayPal as a payment option in addition to your credit card alternatives. Many people think of PayPal as "funny money" and will spend it on whatever they want, including your products.

Another fairly new payment option that some marketers are claiming to get good results from is offering Google Checkout on their site in addition to their regular payment options. If you're using Google AdWords they're offering some interesting processing options based on your level of AdWords spending. It's definitely worth checking out at the least.

Credit cards can be a tricky thing. It's important for you to understand the ins and outs of how they work. Take some time to visit the Newsletter Section of the www.SpeakerFulfillmentServices.com website for an audio download of *"What Information Marketers Need to Know about Merchant Accounts."*

You need to understand discount rates, chargebacks, reserves, and all the other aspects of merchant accounts as they relate to your information marketing business.

MISTAKE #31

NO CONTINUITY OR RECURRING REVENUE STREAMS

Membership sites are hot-hot-hot. Continuity programs, especially forced continuity in some form, are equally hot. If you're an information marketer and you don't have some type of continuity or recurring revenue stream in place, you're losing a lot of money.

As your information marketing business grows, you're going to have a lot of content on your hands. You should have multiple websites, each selling an individual product and producing revenue for you. But, if you're going from sale to sale to build your business, then it's a more difficult process.

What if you placed some or all of your content within a "vault" that users had to pay for monthly to access? Month after month you continue to ding their credit cards for whatever you've set your membership fee and your acquisition cost of that revenue for each succeeding month is zero.

A membership site should be the cornerstone of your information marketing business. To know going into each month how much revenue you're going to generate in advance is powerful. It eases your mind and allows you to focus on growing your business, not just jumping from sale to sale wondering where you'll get your next dollar.

Continuity is a great thing. Automatic billing until you're told to stop can add a tremendous amount of profit to your bottom line. Some of the larger new product launches included a forced continuity component. You receive the "big box" package from the information marketer and part of the package might include a trial membership in their online community. Then, after a couple months you're billed "x" dollars per month unless you drop out.

UPDATE: Credit Card companies typically no longer allows "Forced Continuity" programs. Be sure you know the current regulations prior to trying to implement any type of Forced continuity.

It becomes sort of an "out of sight, out of mind" thing for the users, but if you continue to deliver great new content in your membership area, people will stick—and continue to pay you month after month after month. Gotta love continuity.

MISTAKE #32

NOT HAVING A COACH OR MENTOR OR PARTICIPATING IN A MASTERMIND GROUP

Are you a lone wolf? Do you feel like you have to do it all yourself and that every idea that becomes a part of your business has to come from within your own mind? If you do, then you're probably the biggest barrier your information marketing business has to overcome.

It's been shown time and time again the value of having a coach or mentor or being involved with a mastermind group. Professional athletes have them. The most successful entrepreneurs have them. Great information marketers have them also.

As you work to grow your information marketing business, you'll find the old adage "Can't see the forest for the trees" coming true on a regular basis. You need a fresh perspective—a new set of eyes to help you look at your problems and help you come up with solutions that you couldn't see for yourself.

When you work with a mentor or a coach or a mastermind team, you will benefit in several ways:

- Improve your decision-making ability
- Improve your time management skills

- Sustain focus on your highest priorities
- Make and keep more money
- Reduce isolation, have a supportive person or team for a sounding board and for accountability
- Gain fresh perspectives on problems you are facing

Make sure you use your coach/mentor/mastermind group effectively though. It's important to meet with them on a regular basis, to set clear objectives, to rely upon them for guidance and not answers, to be completely honest, and to remember they're not a dumping ground or place for you to go whine.

Your time and monetary investment in being "coached" should be returned ten fold or more if you take full advantage of it. Your business will grow both faster and stronger if you fully utilize the advantage coaching offers you in your information marketing business.

For information on
Armand Morin's AM2 Internet Coaching Group
visit AM2.com

MISTAKE #33

NOT SPECIALIZED OR NICHED ENOUGH OF A MARKET

The four most dangerous words in the world of selling and marketing probably are, "Everybody needs my product." Talk about a recipe for disaster. In the information marketing industry, it might be phrased as, "If you try to speak to everybody, then you speak to nobody."

As you work to position your product(s) in the marketplace, you've got to determine which sub-segment of the market you want to go after. Too wide of a focus and nobody can relate to your offer because it doesn't speak to them at a level they can relate to.

For example, there are a lot of information products related to time management. If you come out with another generic time-management program, you become just another face in the crowd. You've got to niche your product to a subset of the market looking for help with time management.

How about something like "Time Management for Soccer Moms" or "Time Management for Work at Home Professionals?" When approaching a new market niche it's critical to speak their language. You need to understand the group's "hot buttons" and be ready to communicate with the target market as an understanding member—not as an outsider.

You also need to remember that competition isn't necessarily a bad thing. If you identify a market you think would be hot be sure to do your research first. How many people are looking for information on what you have to offer? If you find no competitors in your segment that in all likelihood means that the market segment isn't profitable enough for others to want to play in.

It can sometimes be a fine line that you walk. You want to be specialized enough that your target market can really relate to your message.

You want them to feel as if you're speaking directly to them. On the other hand, you don't want that market to be so specialized that the size of the market isn't large enough to be profitable for you. But, as a general rule, the more specialized you are, the better off you'll be.

MISTAKE #34

FAILURE TO APPLY ANY "STICK" STRATEGIES

We discussed earlier in the book the subject of helping your customers to "consume" your information via use of autoresponders and a "Read This First" or "Getting Started" document. Both of these tools are designed to help people overcome the "overwhelm" they may feel when they first receive your product—especially if it's a "Big Box" package.

These are just two of many things you can do to help people consume your product and reduce the chances of a product being returned for a refund.

Obviously, it's a given you should deliver high quality content to your customers. But there are a number of other "Stick Strategies" you should employ to help you to reduce refunds and get folks coming back again and again for your information products.

It's all about overcoming buyer's remorse. There's typically a lag period between the initial euphoria of making the decision to purchase your product and the moment the product actually arrives at their door. Doubt begins to creep into their mind—"Have I made a good decision?"

Thousands of products have been returned to our facility where the box was obviously never even opened. If you can't even get them to open your box, how in the world are they going to consume it?

The first thing you should do to help your sales stick is to deliver some content immediately digitally. Get people started quickly consuming your information in some format. You want to avoid the inevitable decrease in enthusiasm for your product that can occur as they wait for the package to arrive. So give them access to some audio content or other component of the product to get the ball rolling.

When the actual box arrives, the first thing your customer should see is a big sticker on this box that says something like "STOP—Before you open this box, call this toll-free number for important information." List an 800 number on the box that goes to a pre-recorded message. That message should reinforce the sale and get them excited about opening the box and digging into your information.

For the current list of recommended, pre-recorded message services, please consult the Recommended Resources section at the end of this book.

This box label is just one of many additional "Stick" strategies you should consider for your products. With appropriate kudos to Alex Mandossian and Joe Polish, here are a few other popular techniques that can help to reduce refunds and keep them coming back for more:

Bonus gift request form—a printed document inside their box they must fax back to claim their bonus items.

Postcard follow-up sequence—a great consumption concept from Alex Mandossian where they receive a physical postcard every week for a few weeks to keep drawing them deeper and deeper into your product, increasing consumption.

Robotic personal coaching—a video or audio postcard message that covers frequently asked questions.

Client newsletters by snail mail—a printed newsletter sent via the postal service that cuts through the clutter and increases customer retention.

Non-relevant gifts—thank you gifts that have nothing to do with your "topic." An example might be brownies, candy, or other consumables branded to you.

For much more detail about the concept of stick strategies, you are encouraged to check out Alex and Joe's excellent course called "*Stick Strategy Secrets.*" Visit the Recommended Resources page at www.50BiggestMistakes.com/Resources to find out if this outstanding course is currently available.

MISTAKE #35

NOT RECOGNIZING THE INFLUENCE WOMEN EXERT IN THE BUYING PROCESS

According to Donna Fox of www.WhySheBuys.com, a staggering 85% of all purchase decisions are controlled by women, and around 94% of all purchase decisions are influenced by women. In addition, 70% OF NEW Internet startups are women owned.

So, what does this mean to you as an information marketer?

If you're selling a "big ticket" information product you need to first be sure that your sales copy isn't overtly slanted towards the male perspective. Most people haven't even considered the impact that women have in the buying process. If you inadvertently upset a key purchasing influence, you'll certainly negatively impact your sales.

Your sales copy may not need changed at all. But, according to Donna, there are six major pillars you need to consider when marketing to women.

#1 Women don't want your marketing to be too "feminine"
#2 Women want answers—the perfect solution to their problem
#3 Women want understanding

#4 Women want convenience

#5 Women want relationships

#6 - Women want the "total package"

So look at your marketing from the perspective of what Donna calls "Inclusive Marketing." Be sure you don't offend women in your copy and try to include sales copy that will address the six pillars.

We talked earlier in this course about "Stick Strategies." Donna talks about a stick strategy she calls the "Wife Acceptance Factor." If you're an information marketer, you will always battle the issue of product returns. On higher priced products, it's fairly common to have a product returned by a male purchaser because "My wife won't let me keep it."

So the stick strategy being employed is to send a separate letter to the wife of the customer reinforcing what a great decision her husband has made and how the product will benefit her. Pure brilliance.

MISTAKE #36

NO UNDERSTANDING OF THE POWER OF EFFECTIVE COPYWRITING

Whether you're selling your information product entirely online or also using offline methods, you should recognize that it's the words that sell your product.

It doesn't matter whether it's a printed sales letter or the copy on a webpage. Words are what do the sales work for you. As an information marketer you'll have to decide which tasks you want to do yourself and which ones you want to outsource or hire people to do for you.

Copywriting is one of those tasks that falls into this realm. Good copywriters are expensive but worth their weight in gold if your financial situation justifies hiring one. It's one of those tasks you should, at the least, have a good understanding of so you can recognize whether you have decent copy or not.

That means you need to educate yourself on copywriting basics to improve your chances for success. Here are some recommended copywriting resources you should consider reading.

- *Scientific Advertising* by Claude Hopkins (Available free online— just do a Google search)
- *Reason Why Advertising Plus Intensive Advertising* by John E. Kennedy
- *How to Write a Good Advertisement* by Vic Schwab
- *How to Write Advertising that Sells* by Clyde Bedell
- *Breakthrough Advertising* by Eugene Schwartz
- *The Robert Collier Letter Book* by Robert Collier
- *The Greatest Direct Mail Sales Letters of All Time* by Richard Hodgson
- *Tested Advertising Methods* by John Caples

For some of the greatest books
ever written on the topics of copywriting
visit our online bookstore at **MarketingClassics.com**

MISTAKE #37

MAKING SURE ANYONE WHO'S WORKING WITH YOU UNDERSTANDS YOUR BRAND AND DOESN'T UNINTENTIONALLY ALIENATE YOUR LIST

I was talking with a colleague at a recent event, and he was telling me the story of how he had worked with a well-known Internet marketer who had crafted an email that was sent out to a list of 60,000 people.

This colleague's list was used to seeing email in a certain style, and the email that was sent had a totally different look, feel and tone. The result? The unsubscribe requests began pouring in one after the other. When all was said and done, a list that had been built up to a nice size of 60,000 was reduced to a meager list of ... just 5,000!

What's the lesson here? It doesn't matter if it's an outside consultant, an employee, a ghostwriter or anyone else doing marketing writing on your behalf, you need to educate them on the format and tone of all your previous email correspondence with your list.

Sometimes a drastic overhaul may be in order. But, if you've built up in your list an expectation of what they're going to see from you and then a communication they receive is incongruent with that expectation, then you may have the disastrous results such as this marketer experienced.

I'm sure there was no malicious intent on the part of the consultant. But obviously they failed to take into account the previous communications and the branding that had been done by this marketer.

If you or someone working on your behalf wants to change your look and feel, you may want to consider doing it in baby steps rather than all at once.

Change things a little bit on the first communication, then a little more on the next message, etc., etc.

Drastic overhauls can create disastrous results. Be careful!

MISTAKE #38

NOT UNDERSTANDING THE POWER OF ARTICLES TO GROW YOUR LIST

To a large extent, the terms "Information Marketing" and "Internet Marketing" have almost become synonymous.

Go to any Internet marketing conference these days and you're likely to hear extensive discussion of information marketing being the perfect Internet business because of the high profit margin on each individual sale.

That means if you're an information marketer you must have full understanding of the most powerful traffic generation tools to get visitors to your website(s). At the top of the list today for many marketers is article marketing.

By providing people with a taste of your content via articles you can stimulate them to want to visit your website for more information about that topic.

Take advantage of the low or no cost article submission services available to you like EzineArticles.com, SubmitYourArticle.com, and ArticleMarketer.com to get your articles distributed in as many appropriate venues as possible as quickly as possible.

The key to gaining maximum benefit from article marketing is to have a well crafted resource box at the end of the article. According to article marketing expert Christopher Knight of www.Christopher-Knight.com the following items are mandatory in your resource box:

- Your name
- Your website address in valid URL form. For example http://Your-Company-Name.com
- Your elevator pitch—1 to 3 sentences that encapsulate the essence of what makes you and your offering unique.
- Your call to action—In addition, your resource box might include your ezine subscription address, your contact information, a free report, and an anchor URL that is related to one keyword or keyword phrase you want to build SEO strength for.

The body of your article is where you "give" and the resource box is where you "take" for your article marketing gift of information.

Be sure to include the mandatory elements described above to gain the maximum benefits of article marketing.

MISTAKE #39

NOT UTILIZING ALL OF YOUR PRODUCT "REAL ESTATE" TO SELL MORE TO YOUR CUSTOMERS

We discussed earlier the importance of building email capture tools within the content of your information product to help build your list so you can market additional products and services to your customers.

When our company, Speaker Fulfillment Services, is working with a new client, one of the biggest mistakes I see them make is not taking full advantage of their product real estate to sell more to their customers.

Here's a specific example that I see all the time, and I cringe every time I see it.

A new course is developed that includes a manual or workbook that is either spiral bound or placed within a three-ring binder. We receive the artwork for the binder from our client, and they have only a front and spine outsert for their binder—no back.

This is prime real estate that you need to take advantage of. You can use it to sell other products. Or you can use it as a stick strategy where you include testimonials or other information they will reinforce the value of the information your customer has just purchased from you.

Here's a starter list of what all you might include on this valuable real estate:

- Testimonials from customers, especially well-known centers of influence
- A description of other products or services you have to offer and a call to action to drive them back to a website for more information
- Short biographies of key contributors to your product that will further substantiate the value of the purchase in your customer's mind

When people pick up a book in a bookstore, what do they frequently do first? They flip it over and read the back copy. Your information products should be approached in the same way. Use the back for advertising/sales copy, and you'll increase your overall sales.

MISTAKE #40

NOT ADDRESSING ALL THE LEARNING MODALITIES BY WHICH PEOPLE CONSUME INFORMATION

There are four basic types of learners in this world. In simple terms, these can be classified as readers, listeners, watchers, and doers.

Some people classify readers as what they call "tactile" learners—these are the people who learn by touching i.e. books or home study courses.

Your listeners can also be called "auditory" learners—they learn primarily by listening to audio content. This can be in the form of CDs, teleseminars, or podcasts as possible examples.

Watchers are your "visual" learners. They are great prospects for delivery by DVD or webinars.

And the fourth group is your doers. They learn kinesthetically, which means they want to be involved in the process rather than just watching, listening, or reading about it.

But what does all this mean to you as an information marketer? It means that if you're not offering your content in a variety of formats then you're at best overlooking part of your potential audience and at worst alienating them.

We talked earlier in this course the importance of repurposing content. It can't be emphasized enough how critical it is for you to repurpose. First, from the standpoint of lightening your workload—you don't want to have to create from scratch every time. But secondly, and probably more important, is that it allows you to cover all the learning styles your customers use fairly easily.

Here's a quick example. This book is offered with the written content you're reading right now, as well as the audio recording, so you can listen if you'd prefer that to reading.

Each chapter is also being recorded as a quick and dirty two-minute video that's being posted on YouTube and other video sites to drive traffic to our primary company website.

The same video can also be used within a membership site as additional content. Each chapter is also being turned into an article and submitted to the various article directories.

So we're repurposing the content for both marketing and content delivery purposes, while at the same time we're addressing the different learning modalities that exist in the marketplace.

MISTAKE #41

TREATING YOUR INFORMATION MARKETING AS A HOBBY RATHER THAN A BUSINESS

Don't even think about kidding yourself on this one. If you want to treat information marketing as a hobby, that's your choice, but if you want to really make it big and succeed as an information marketer, then you need to treat your information marketing endeavors as a business, not a hobby.

Billions of dollars per year are made in the information marketing industry. That's billions with a "*b.*" If you want a bigger slice of this pie, then you have to think like a business thinks. How are you going to handle all of the following?

- Sales
- Marketing
- Product Development
- Accounting
- Asset Protection
- Distribution
- Manufacturing
- Human Resources

- Information Technology
- Purchasing
- Customer Service

Every business is comprised of hundreds of little processes and procedures. Everything you do can have minor or major repercussions elsewhere in your organization. Disciplined thought is frequently required to make sure you're not making some potentially catastrophic decision.

Sound scary? Maybe. But what's scarier is having a business suddenly take off and you not having the infrastructure, processes, and procedures in place to support that growth.

What if you unexpectedly hit a "home run" with some new product you come out with? Can your organization withstand the onslaught of product delivery and customer support that will be required to support that? You can truly become a victim of your own success if you haven't planned appropriately for what might happen.

Remember, if you're doing it right, you're running an information marketing business, not an information-marketing hobby.

MISTAKE #42

NOT UNDERSTANDING THE LIFETIME VALUE OF A CUSTOMER AND HOW MUCH YOU CAN AFFORD TO SPEND TO ACQUIRE A NEW CUSTOMER

If you don't know these numbers, you don't know anything. You're totally shooting in the dark with your information marketing business when you have no idea of what marketing channels are working for you and what the cost of acquiring a new customer is and what that customer is worth to you over their lifetime.

I first learned about the concept of lifetime customer value from marketing legend Jay Abraham in the mid-1990s. While we're talking about the information marketing business, understanding of this concept is essential to any type of business.

The basic calculation of Lifetime Customer Value is a simple one. Just divide your revenue over time by the number of customers who generated that revenue. That gives you the average lifetime value of a customer to you.

You can use that figure to determine how much you can afford to spend to acquire a new customer. I think it's more important to think of this in terms of the profitability of a customer rather than just the gross sales revenue. If you have hard costs associated with making a sale those should be taken into account before deciding the justifiable new customer acquisition cost you can afford to absorb.

You should also remember to segregate your customer list in different ways as part of your analysis process. Customers who participate in a continuity program of yours may have greater value than others. Or people that attend live events may be of greater value.

You should also look at your various lead generation sources. You may find that one particular marketing channel generates far more valuable customers to you than another. Or you might find certain socio-economic groups, or countries, or sex, or ethnic group might generate higher value customers.

Know these numbers. It's critical to your long-term success.

MISTAKE #43

A WEAK OR NON-EXISTENT GUARANTEE

You're competing with lots of other products in the marketplace. The person reading your sales letter, whether online or offline probably has doubts about your claims and wonders whether your product will really work for them or not.

We'll talk later about the power of testimonials to help overcome these doubts. But, aside from testimonials one of the biggest weapons in your marketing arsenal should be a strong guarantee.

You need to place the risk of loss for purchasing your product on yourself rather than the customer. Risk reversal removes that risk of loss from your customer, whether they need to justify their purchase to a spouse, business partner, or just within their own mind, and places it squarely back on you.

You remove that risk with your guarantee. If a customer buys your product and it doesn't meet their needs they can return it for a refund. You'll have to decide how long your guarantee period should be and whether it's going to be a conditional or unconditional guarantee.

Take a look at what others in the market are doing. Your merchant account provider will be extremely interested in your guarantee. The longer your guarantee period the less they will like it because it increases their potential exposure for a longer period. 30 to 45 day periods are the norm in the industry, but you'll have to decide what works best for you.

Will you have the occasional buyer who takes advantage of your guarantee? Sure you will. Just consider it a cost of doing business. The additional sales you generate from having a strong guarantee will more than offset the refunds you may have to issue to dishonest people.

MISTAKE #44

FAILING TO COVER ALL THE LEGAL REQUIREMENTS OF INFORMATION MARKETING

Within the last few years a very well known and highly successful information marketer had his business shut down by the Federal Trade Commission because, as I understand it, they felt his earnings claims on his website were overstated or something to that effect.

Shock waves were felt throughout the information-marketing world. If this super marketer, who everyone felt was above board, could be hauled down by the FTC, then was everyone's information marketing business in danger?

Not to worry, the information marketing business is alive and well. While the situation a few years ago created a lot of pain for this one person, the overall impact on the industry was good. It caused information marketers to make sure they were accurate in their claims and to make sure they dotted all their i's and crossed all their t's in regards to what information they placed on their websites.

Did you know that the U.S. Food and Drug Administration has specific rules about weight loss offers? Whatever industry you're operating in, you should be aware of any legal requirements about what you can and can't do in your marketing.

When you're researching a niche market part of your research MUST include what regulatory issues, if any, you'll have to deal with in that particular industry.

Any testimonials you have on your website should be documented. You must be able to prove that the claims made are true with the documentation to back up that claim available. Any testimonials or claims made in your marketing materials are viewed by the FTC as if you actually wrote them yourself.

Your must also now make sure you state the "average results" a purchaser of your product or service will achieve.

On your website, there is some information that should be standard. This includes:

- Warranties, Disclaimer, and Legal Rights
- Earnings Disclaimer
- Terms of Service
- Privacy Policy

There's an excellent software product called AutoWebLaw available for less than $100 that helps you with some of the legal aspects of your information marketing business. For more info visit the Resources section at www.50BiggestMistakes.com/Resources for more information.

Bottom line—just be aware and do the things you need to do to cover your own butt.

MISTAKE #45

NOT KEEPING YOUR MERCHANT ACCOUNT PROVIDER IN THE LOOP PRIOR TO A NEW PRODUCT LAUNCH

When you set up a merchant account in order to accept credit cards, you're typically required to provide information such as what will be your average ticket price, what your high-ticket price will be, and what you expect your monthly sales volume to be.

Your provider will monitor your account to see that you're staying in or near the original numbers you specified when setting up your account. If you suddenly process orders way outside your "norms," then warning bells go off with your provider, and they tend to get a little nervous.

So, let's say you normally process $30,000 per month through your merchant account. Then you do a new product launch and sell over $1,000,000 of a product within just a few day period. Don't you think that's going to raise a few eyebrows in the offices of your merchant account provider?

You bet it will. Your provider doesn't know what you've done to generate all that extra money, and they're concerned about their potential liability. What can they do? They can freeze a large portion of your money for up to six months to make sure they're covered in the event of heavy refunds or chargebacks.

Armand Morin tells the story of how a few years ago his first big online "home run" generated 4.2 million in sales within just a few weeks. And then how he had $2 million of that money "hijacked" by the merchant account provider for six months because the volume was way outside the norms. He eventually received all his money, and I'm sure we'd all like to have this kind of a problem. But what if you had affiliate commissions to pay and production costs to pay that totaled up to more than half of the money you took in?

You'd have, at minimum, a real embarrassing situation on your hands.

Be sure to keep in close communication with your merchant account provider prior to any new product launches. If you keep them in the loop, you'll significantly minimize your chances of having problems like this occur.

Our recommended resource for a
merchant account is PowerPay.
For complete details go to:
InfoMarketingMerchantAccount.com

MISTAKE #46

FAILING TO PROVIDE ENOUGH PROOF THROUGH TESTIMONIALS

When you begin to sell your information product, you know you're going to have to overcome the natural disbelief the market will have regarding what your product will do for them.

Tools available to help include: case studies, physical demonstrations, pictures, financial statements, and testimonials. Of these, testimonials can be the most powerful weapon in your arsenal.

Testimonials are so important because what others say about you is ten times more believable then what you might say about yourself. And the best kind of testimonial is a "specific results" testimonial. That means your customers explains in detail the specific results he/she achieved as a result of using your product.

These results could be dollars earned, percentage increases in business, or any number of other things. The more specific the better. 92.7% increase in sales is way more believable than saying more than 90%.

$34,997.98 in sales last month will serve you far better than saying over $34,000 in sales. Specifics help sell, generalities don't.

Online, video testimonials are the most powerful form because people can see and hear your customer in addition to reading the written comments.

But you should also use audio testimonials and written testimonials. And you should include them in your outgoing product shipments as part of your stick strategies.

Testimonials should, at the least, identify the customer by full name and city and state. Online you might also find the URL of the commenter. If you choose to list the URL make sure it's not an active link so you don't risk leading the reader off your website.

According to Jack Trout in *The New Positioning*, a testimonial attacks the insecure mind on several emotional fronts—"a trifecta of vanity, jealousy, and fear of being left out."

You really can't overdo it on testimonials. Internet marketer Marlon Sanders has hundreds of product testimonials on his website. A disc full of testimonials is frequently included by information marketers, along with offline sales letters.

Testimonials are a must in your marketing.

Recommended Resource for Audio Testimonials
AudioGenerator.com.
Provides you a toll-free call-in number you can give to your clients so they can give you audio testimonials you can use on your website.

MISTAKE #47

NOT MANAGING YOUR LIST PROPERLY

Your list may be your greatest business asset. A well-maintained list that you've built a real relationship with is your single greatest business asset. So why do so many people manage their lists so poorly?

To build a real relationship with your list you've got to provide them content of value. It's fine to make an offer to your list from time to time. In fact, it's foolish if you don't monetize your list in some way. But if you do nothing but try and sell your list constantly you'll turn them off and unsubscribe requests will become more frequent.

If you're working in multiple market niches it's critical to keep your lists properly segmented. You should be providing content and making offers that relate to the area of interest of that particular list. Your cat lovers list members probably aren't going to be interested in your special sale of doggie collars.

Regular communication is also a very important factor. Out of sight, out of mind certainly applies in this situation. Every week that goes by, without some communication from you, causes your list to grow colder and colder and colder.

Some marketers claim you can't email too often as long as you're providing valuable content along the way.

MISTAKE #48

NOT RECOGNIZING THE FULL POWER OF OUTSOURCING AND APPLYING OTHER BUSINESS AMPLIFIERS TO HELP YOU GROW MORE QUICKLY

As you work to grow your information marketing business, if you think you can do it all yourself, you're only kidding yourself. We talked earlier about outsourcing of your product duplication and fulfillment needs, but that's only one of many needs you may have that can be outsourced to help you grow your business even faster.

Just use the list below to stimulate your thinking on how you can use outsourcing to help your grow your business. This list is a summary of services provided by the well-known outsourcing firm Workaholics4Hire.com.

- Viability research
- eBook development
- Content writing (reports, blogs, articles, product reviews, etc.)
- In depth research to locate products to sell
- Transcribing audio or video
- Customer support solutions
- Blog creation and customization

- Webmaster on call
- Article marketing
- Blog comment marketing
- Discussion-board buzz marketing
- Blog directory submission
- Free classifieds marketing
- Press release marketing
- Pay per click campaign management

Virtual assistants are available to handle the routine tasks that can allow you to focus your efforts on the more valuable activities of sales and marketing and product creation. Services like eLance, Rent-a-Coder, and ScriptLance can be utilized to help with product creation. Ghostwriters can write content for you.

Outsourcing isn't the only business "amplifier" available to you. At some point in time, it may make sense to hire an actual employee. Also, software tools can be considered business "amplifiers." A software tool that allows you to automate a process that saves you time on a regular basis is also a business amplifier.

Business amplifiers, including outsourcing, can be valuable assets to help you grow your information marketing empire.

MISTAKE #49

DEVELOPING ANOTHER "ME TOO" INTERVIEW PRODUCT THAT'S SOLD IN A "ME TOO" WAY

The Internet marketing industry is filled with what I call "me too" information products. Someone does an interview series with a group of experts and launches that product to the market.

Someone else sees what they're doing, thinks it's a great idea, and does their own interview series. And so on and so on. Soon the market is filled with dozens of versions of essentially the same product. How's one to stand out in the crowd?

The key is to not have just another "me too" product sold the same way as everything else. You've got to find a "hook" or "angle" that sets your product apart from the other products on the same subject. You've got to have a good story to tell.

In markets outside the Internet marketing arena, interview products have been used very little. You may still have an opportunity in many markets to get what's called the "First Mover Advantage." If you've lost that advantage, your challenge is to differentiate yourself in some way in order to be able to compete.

Good marketing is what can set a "me too" product apart from the crowd. If you want to do another "me too" product, that's your choice. But remember, the best product doesn't win, the best-marketed product does.

MISTAKE #50

LOTS OF IDEAS, LITTLE IMPLEMENTATION

One of the services our company has provided over the last several years is handling the sales table at various Internet and information marketing conferences. As a result, we've seen more than our share of what are called "seminar junkies."

While we talked earlier about the importance of attending live events to network, nothing pains me more than to see the same person repeatedly coming to the sales table purchasing package after package.

They jump from idea to idea, looking for some "magic bullet" that doesn't exist. Every idea sounds like the best idea they ever heard. Ideas are great, but implementation is where it's at. If you never take action on what you learn and never bring your product to market, then you make nothing from the idea.

Good ideas truly are a dime a dozen. Great implementation is worth more than its weight in gold. Nike says, "Just Do It." Larry the Cable Guys says, "Git 'R Done." However you say it, if you never lay that first brick, you'll never build your information marketing empire.

Implementation is It. Implementation is It. Implementation is It. Are you up to It?

MISTAKE #51

NOT TAPPING INTO THE POWER OF EBAY AS A LEAD GENERATION TOOL

eBay is like an invisible 800-pound gorilla to most people in the information marketing industry. Yet, those that tap into the marketing muscle of this giant can use it to quickly build their list.

Millions of people use eBay every day. I've heard that eBay has surpassed nearly every, if not all, major search engines for the number of searches performed.

So, how can you use eBay to help you build your information marketing business? The real key is to use it as a lead generation tool. Offer a front end product at almost no cost with a "Buy It Now" option. The names you capture will help you to build your list.

These are more valuable names because they've spent something in order to get your information. They have a definite interest in your topic because they've spoken with their wallets at some level.

Your real money is obviously in the back end. Once you've gotten them into your sales funnel you can begin to offer them your higher priced products and services outside the framework of eBay.

The top searched items on eBay are for things people are looking to buy. On general search engines people are usually just seeking information. So you can see why these would be better qualified leads for you.

Figure out some way to make eBay a lead generation tool for you information marketing business. It'll be well worth your while.

MISTAKE #52

NOT RECOGNIZING THE POWER OF TELESEMINARS AND WEBINARS AS SALES AND CONTENT DEVELOPMENT TOOLS

In the last few years, perhaps nothing has had as big of an impact on the world of information marketing as the mighty Teleseminar. You can now expand this to include the ever more popular Webinar.

Either format enables you to deliver your message from the comfort of your home or from anywhere on the road to your audience. Whether it's for purposes of a sales call or for content delivery, teleseminars or webinars give you the ability to reach a wider audience more quickly.

Teleseminars or webinars can be used both as revenue generators as well as content development tools, or some combination thereof. They can be sold as single calls or as a series. They can be sold with or without transcripts in PDF or printed form.

A significant factor in your success with teleseminars and webinars will be your ability to get those people that have signed up for a call to show up for the call. If they're not there then it's impossible to sell them anything if revenue generation is the way you're using them.

Alex Mandossian teaches in his highly regarded Teleseminar Secrets course several strategies for getting those who have signed up for an event to actually show up. Frequent email reminders and "Print This Now" documents are only a couple of the tools available to increase attendance on teleseminars and webinars.

In an earlier section, we talked about repurposing content. Teleseminars may be your best way to create original content that you can then use any number of different ways to build your information marketing empire.

INFORMATION MARKETER'S RESOURCE ROLODEX

For the current list of recommended resources in the following areas, please go online to www.50BiggestMistakes.com/Resources.

- Audio Equipment for Creating Content
- Audio Recording/Editing
- Coaching Groups
- Copywriters
- Digital Product Protection
- Duplication and Fulfillment
- eBook Software
- eCover Software
- Graphic Artists
- Information Marketing Blogs
- Legal Software
- Membership Sites
- Merchant Accounts
- Online Testing
- Pre-recorded Message 800 Number Services
- Recommended Training Products
- Survey Tools
- Testimonials Service
- Transcription
- Virtual Assistants
- Website Software

THANK YOU

Thank you for reading the *50 Biggest Mistakes I See Information Marketers Make*. I hope the information shared in this book will help you to avoid many information-marketing mistakes and grow your business faster, stronger, and with fewer headaches than you could have ever imagined.

Your comments on this course would be most appreciated. Please send your testimonials via email to Comments@50BiggestMistakes.com. Or, if you'd prefer to leave a voice testimonial, please call our toll-free testimonial line at 800-609-9006 ext. 1669.

If you're ever in need of information product duplication and/or fulfillment, I hope you'll consider Speaker Fulfillment Services. For more information about our services, please visit our homepage, along with any of these other Bret Ridgway associated sites:

- SpeakerFulfillmentServices.com
- SFSBlog.com
- SFSRecommends.com
- MarketingClassics.com
- 50BiggestMistakes.com
- AM2.com
- Infofillment.com
- 50BiggestWebsiteMistakes.com
- RedOakCart.com
- Client.Infofillment.com
- LeadGenDiscs.com

ABOUT BRET

 Bret Ridgway, along with business partner Bryan Hane, are co-founders of Speaker Fulfillment Services, a company that provides authors, speakers, and information marketers with product duplication and fulfillment services from their home base in Terre Haute, Indiana. You can contact by email at bret@sfsmail.com.

BUY A SHARE OF THE FUTURE IN YOUR COMMUNITY

These certificates make great holiday, graduation and birthday gifts that can be personalized with the recipient's name. The cost of one S.H.A.R.E. or one square foot is $54.17. The personalized certificate is suitable for framing and will state the number of shares purchased and the amount of each share, as well as the recipient's name. The home that you participate in "building" will last for many years and will continue to grow in value.

HABITAT FOR HUMANITY

THIS CERTIFIES THAT

YOUR NAME HERE

HAS INVESTED IN A HOME FOR A DESERVING FAMILY

1985-2005

TWENTY YEARS OF BUILDING FUTURES IN OUR
COMMUNITY ONE HOME AT A TIME

1200 SQUARE FOOT HOUSE @ $65,000 = $54.17 PER SQUARE FOOT
This certificate represents a tax deductible donation. It has no cash value.

Here is a sample SHARE certificate:

YES, I WOULD LIKE TO HELP!

*I support the work that Habitat for Humanity does and I want to be part of the excitement! As a donor, I will receive periodic updates on your construction activities but, more importantly, I know my gift will help a family in our community realize the dream of homeownership. **I would like to SHARE in your efforts against substandard housing in my community!** (Please print below)*

PLEASE SEND ME _____ SHARES at $54.17 EACH = $ $_____

In Honor Of: _____

Occasion: (Circle One)   *HOLIDAY*   *BIRTHDAY*   *ANNIVERSARY*

      OTHER: _____

Address of Recipient: _____

Gift From: _____ *Donor Address:* _____

Donor Email: _____

I AM ENCLOSING A CHECK FOR $ $_____ PAYABLE TO HABITAT FOR HUMANITY <u>OR</u> PLEASE CHARGE MY VISA OR MASTERCARD *(CIRCLE ONE)*

Card Number _____ Expiration Date: _____

Name as it appears on Credit Card _____ Charge Amount $ _____

Signature _____

Billing Address _____

Telephone # Day _____ Eve _____

PLEASE NOTE: Your contribution is tax-deductible to the fullest extent allowed by law.
Habitat for Humanity • P.O. Box 1443 • Newport News, VA 23601 • 757-596-5553
www.HelpHabitatforHumanity.org